# GETTING INTO
# PRO FOOTBALL

# GETTING INTO PRO
# FOOTBALL

## BY JOHN D. McCALLUM

GETTING INTO THE PROS
FRANKLIN WATTS • NEW YORK • LONDON • 1979

Photograph on page 39 courtesy of the University of Washington. Photograph on page 67 courtesy of the Seattle Seahawks. Photographs on pages 27, 33, 54, 55, and 78 courtesy of Wide World Photos. All other photographs courtesy of United Press International.

Library of Congress Cataloging in Publication Data

McCallum, John Dennis, 1924–
    Getting into pro football.

    (Getting into the pros)
    Includes index.
    SUMMARY: Offers tips on diet, drugs, mental conditioning, exercise, choosing a college, winning a scholarship, and other topics for those who choose to enter professional football.
    1.  Football—Vocational guidance—Juvenile literature. [1. Football—Vocational guidance. 2. Vocational guidance] I. Title.
GV950.7.M3        796.33′2′023        78–23452
ISBN 0–531–02279–X

# CONTENTS

**To**
a couple of
genuine pros,
Don and Fran
Pugnetti


"Pro football is the
toughest way I know to
make an easy buck."

—Norm Van Brocklin

# GETTING INTO PRO FOOTBALL

# THE WINNING
# ATTITUDE

Sixty years ago, University of Michigan Coach Fielding H. Yost was asked what he thought of a proposal to credit football teams with one point for each first down, in addition to the points scored by touchdowns, conversions, field goals, and safeties.

"Well," Hurry-Up Yost said, "you'd still have a game. Of course, it wouldn't be football—but you'd still have a game."

Fortunately, football is still football. Granted it is much more technical than it was back in its beginnings. Players are bigger and faster, taught to be far more specialized and less individualistic, and, particularly if the player is a quarterback, packed with a lot more play information. But, all in all, football remains very much the same old crowd-pleaser. It is still great fun to watch and great fun to play.

What is it that makes a football champion? Certainly physical ability is part of it. Yet how many times have you seen a player of exceptional physical potential fail to develop into a champion? Calisthenics can build the body. Courses of study can train the mind. But the real champion is the person whose attitude is right. But what is the right attitude?

First of all, being able to deal with failure is part

of it. Champions are usually those who have failed not just once, but many times; failed and found out that it wasn't the end of the world.

The potential champion is the person who doesn't fall apart when a mistake happens. The champion develops a feel for pressure; he becomes clutchworthy.

Some people seem to think that winning always means winning the game, that if you don't win the game you are a loser. Actually, if you are ever going to be a winner you must first have a winning attitude.

For you as a player to develop the proper winning atttitude, there must be a healthy relationship between you and your coach. Your success may hinge on whether or not you respect your coach. This is one thing a coach must keep in mind constantly. He has to be consistent on and off the field to hold your respect.

Along with respect comes discipline. If you respect your coach you'll generally accept his discipline.

Self-discipline, too, is important at all levels of football. Say, for instance, that you are a very promising player, a true pro prospect, and you know it. While recognizing your talent, the coach also sees that you are star-struck. He is concerned. Your attitude toward the team and your teammates and the effort you are making are far below par. The coach's problem is this: Does he tolerate your conduct or does he wash you out after warning you to mend your ways? Coaches are faced with this situation all the time. The solution is usually quite simple. Anybody who lacks self-disci-

**The game of football being played by one of the best, Joe Namath (center).**

**Vince Lombardi gets a victory ride from the Green Bay Packers after their win in the 1968 Super Bowl.**

pline, who doesn't want to be part of the team, who doesn't want to meet the requirements, has to go. For the good of the team, there is no other way.

Former Oklahoma Coach Bud Wilkinson, who signed as head coach of the NFL St. Louis Cardinals in 1978, says that the only competition worth very much is competition with yourself. "This gets back to the point about winning," he said. "Winning or losing is important as far as the score is concerned. You can't wash it out. But I think this is a result, not necessarily the objective. If a coach is able to get the very best out of his players, given any kind of competition, he wins by default. The other people are not able to do it."

Not many occupations bring together fighting and working the way football does. Linebacker Ray Mansfield, an All-American at the University of Washington and then a star in the NFL, agrees with Coach Wilkinson's theories on winning and losing, only he talks as one who has fought in a war. "Don't ever, ever, accept getting beat," he tells recruits. "Don't ever let a guy beat you and walk away and say, 'Well, he beat me.' You have to fight and scratch and bite. If you're bleeding and crying and scratching, keep on fighting and that guy will quit. As long as *you* don't."

One of the most quoted lines in sports was made by Vince Lombardi: "Winning isn't everything, it's the *only* thing." He also said, "If you can shrug off a loss, you can't be a winner. The harder you work, the harder it is to lose."

And so the question to you is: How hard are you willing to work at football? How far you go in the game depends on your answer. High school ball? College? The NFL? Before you say the last, consider the odds. Out of an estimated ten thousand candidates each year only *one* is signed to a National Football League contract. Even if you are invited to try out, the odds are still against you. Professional teams march off to their preseason training camps in July with 100 to 110 players—and then the squad cuts begin. Within the first two weeks, the number per team drops to seventy candidates; the next week they drop to sixty. They stay in the sixty-fifty range for a few more weeks, before the final roster drops to forty-three. It is thus indeed a very tight funnel that you drop into. Why some players make it and others don't has a lot to do with being at the right place at the right time. It is that close.

Vince Lombardi put it so well. He once pointed out that there are approximately 160 plays in a football game, but only three or four make a difference in determining the outcome of the game. "But you never know when those three or four plays are coming," he said. "So you have to put out on all 160 of them, because it may be the first or the last play that breaks open the game."

Because the percentage of college players who make it in professional football is so small, perhaps you should make a career in pro ball a *desire,* not a goal. A goal is something you intend to attain. You can attain goals and keep reaching for higher goals. But when you talk about football, you are talking about millions of boys who play it every year—down to the hundreds who win honors of various kinds—down to the few who are drafted by the pros—down to the fewer yet who actually make the NFL teams.

Whatever your destiny in football, always try to be the very best player you can. Enjoy whatever success you have in high school and college football. If your talents develop adequately, then the world of professional football awaits you. If not, at least you will know in your heart that you have tried.

# SHAPING UP: DIET, DRUGS, AND MENTAL CONDITIONING

Vince Lombardi believed in physical fitness and proper conditioning. He was always talking about "fourth-quarter shape."

"The last five or six games of the schedule most teams are just plain pooped, playing all worn out, and can be easily hurt," he said. "A team will come down to the last five games, its players are dragging their butts, and they will win or lose because the quarterback has a hot hand that afternoon or a cold one. A team simply cannot play twenty games in that kind of shape. The body gives out. It isn't in *fourth-quarter shape.* And so you're forced to watch the Super Bowl from a seat in the grandstand."

Jack Youngblood, who played a lot of defensive end for the Los Angeles Rams in 1977, thinks of his body as a test tube. "You have to put in exactly the right ingredients to get the best reaction out of it," he says. "Nutrition is an essential element for any athlete."

Says Dr. Timothy T. Craig, a pioneer in the American Medical Association's division of sports medicine: "Athletes who are concerned with diet are naturally looking at it from a performance point of view; they look for an elixir to give them a slight advantage over their opponents." Accordingly, most athletic diets reflect a greater than normal concern for proper nutrition. Most athletes consider food to be fuel.

Jack Youngblood is in the best of shape. "My favorite dinner is steamed broccoli, a piece of broiled halibut, and one of my wife's great Italian salads," he revealed. "I can't eat beef. It's too rich, too acidic. Broiled or boiled chicken is good for me, and lots of fish. The normal American diet of steak, potatoes, ice cream, and white bread is a killer. That's heart attack and stroke country. The trick is to find out how little your body can do with, then stay there."

Then there is Fred Dryer, who eats meat about once a week. "It's not because I'm a health-food freak or an organics guy," he says, "but because I'm convinced from my own investigation that meat is an inefficient means of getting protein. It's like white bread. Some guy along the line thought, 'Ooh, look at this ratty, ugly brown wheat. Let's bleach it until it's sweet and white and all clean.' So they make white bread, taking out all the nutrients and fiber. To prove how fresh it is, you squeeze it—like this." Dryer demonstrated by bringing his huge hands together until there was only enough room left inside for a walnut. "And that's what it does in your intestines."

Dryer lives on two meals a day that include little meat and no white bread. "About 8 a.m., I have eight raw egg yolks, milk, applesauce, papaya juice, and two

**Above: Jack Youngblood shouting with joy after a dramatic 14–12 win over Dallas in the NFC 1976 playoffs. Below: Fred Dryer (left) in a game against the Buffalo Bills.**

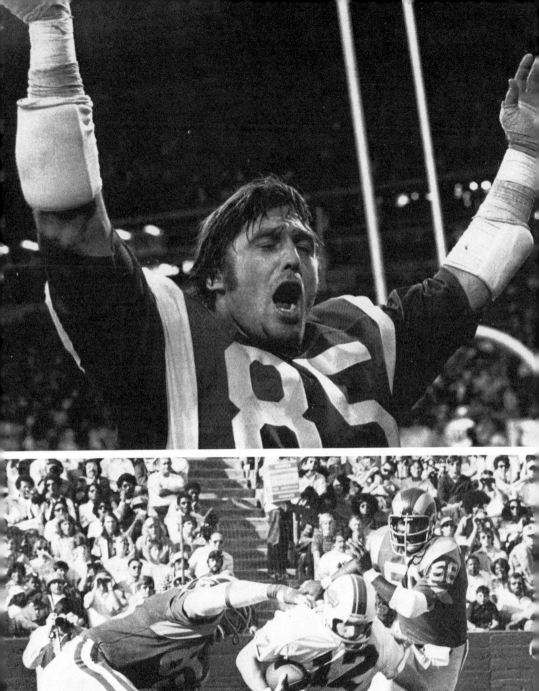

tablespoons of bran, all mixed in a blender," he said. "Then about 6 p.m., I steam up ten or twelve different vegetables and eat two or three bowlsful of that. If I'm hungry at night, I have another one of those cocktails."

Well, what should an athlete eat? There are almost as many opinions on that question as there are football players. Physiologist Joan Ullyot, a doctor who specializes in sports medicine at the Institute of Health Research in San Francisco, determined in a study of more than one thousand healthy persons that the healthiest among them were vegetarians who run. The next healthiest were non-running vegetarians, followed by runners who eat an ordinary diet, then non-runners on an ordinary diet. It's not surprising, then, that Dr. Ullyot recommends that athletes go on a vegetarian diet, one that includes eggs and milk products.

"I suggest starting the day with a breakfast of whole grain cereal and fruit," she said. "For lunch or dinner, I recommend vegetable soup, a salad, cottage cheese, and perhaps even a little fish. For snacks, there's nothing better than whole grain bread slathered with natural peanut butter and washed down with a glass of milk. A lot of football players are scared to go on a vegetarian diet because they think they won't get enough protein, but that's not true. There's nothing you get from meat that you can't get from a good vegetarian diet. For bulk and endurance, an athlete should fill up on carbohydrates—spaghetti, lasagna, potatoes. Professional athletes often have the misconception that you have to build yourself up with lots of protein. That's a ridiculous idea. You need carbohydrates as fuel to provide all the energy you are using."

"The main obstacle to most players adopting such a diet," she says, "is the advice they get from trainers and coaches all during their years in high school and college. Any coach who believes steak and eggs are best is behind the times."

Dr. Beverly Bullen, director of Boston University's graduate program in nutrition, offers a diet of more familiar fare. Her recommendation is for "a generally balanced diet—vegetables, meat, carbohydrates, and so on—with enough calories to cover the rigors of training."

That's simple enough, but Dr. Bullen adds a few warnings. Eat poultry and fish for the high-grade protein that the athlete needs and cannot get from strictly vegetarian fare, but go easy on steak, because it has too much fat. Drink skim milk fortified with Vitamins A and D rather than whole milk with its high-fat content.

"Everyone is eating too much fat," Dr. Bullen says. "Even high protein consumption can cause trouble. The more animal protein a person eats the more urea he or she produces, making the kidneys work harder. The result in some cases is serious kidney damage. However, if eating a lot of meat psychs a player up and convinces him that it will help his game, then I guess it's all right, so long as someone makes certain it isn't causing him any injury. In any case, an athlete should never eat a high-protein or fat-heavy meal within four hours of competition, because it takes too long to digest."

Gary Nicholson, whose career as an athletic trainer includes stints at Indiana University, Pacific Lutheran University, the Chicago Cubs, and the Seattle Mariners, has some very definite opinions about diet, sleep and rest, drugs and stimulants, and mental conditioning.

"The proper approach to a training diet is balance and moderation," he told me. "An athlete who eats at home, in the dormitory, or at a training table usually receives a substantial, well-balanced meal. He should avoid exceptionally greasy foods and any others that he has found to disagree with him. During the competitive season the athlete must avoid experimenting with new foods. This is especially true on days of competition and on trips where new and inviting dishes are listed on hotel or restaurant menus. It is well to remember that the athlete, as a rule, needs almost twice as many calories as the non-athlete. A total of 3,500 to 4,500 calories per day is usually required by the average pro football player.

"On game day the athlete should eat sparingly. In no case should he eat later than three or four hours before competition. That meal should consist of bland, nourishing food in moderate portions. All food should be chewed well to promote thorough digestion. Proper consumption of water is also necessary. This is especially true on game days, so that the players do not waterlog themselves prior to the game. Water should be sipped, not gulped, and should not be taken in large quantities. When sipped, the cold fluid is warmed before it reaches the digestive tract."

Gary Nicholson also has some very definite ideas about other training habits.

*Drugs and stimulants.* "Tobacco and alcohol are two of the most common means of dissipation. The athlete should not use either. A cigarette or a drink has never improved the condition of any athlete. In fact, several studies have shown that the use of tobacco or alcohol hinders top physical performance. The detrimental effect upon the athlete may be mental or physical or both."

*Mental conditioning.* "Without exception, mental fatigue sets in before physical fatigue. Even the greatest of athletes thinks he is tired before his body is really physically tired. Training and conditioning programs should recognize this problem. Often the athlete can overcome this 'feeling of being tired' and perform much closer to *real* capacity. Proper and well-directed training builds confidence, and confidence is a great factor in the struggle against feeling mentally fatigued. Another factor to deal with is the warm-up. Failure to warm up properly usually leads to an early sensation of fatigue, because the body has not been prepared physiologically for the work it is doing. The sensation of second wind is usually experienced by undertrained athletes, or by those who have failed to warm up properly."

*Sleep and rest.* "When you talk about proper rest for athletes, my advice is for them to live their normal day-to-day life. Some players before a big game say, 'Well, I need a couple hours extra rest to prepare for the game.' So they sleep a little longer or lie down to take a nap and they get up feeling sluggish, listless, slow. The number of hours of sleep required depends on the individual athlete. One person might need seven hours of sleep on the eve of a game, another might require ten. Pregame jitters might cause still others to lose sleep. What concerns me most about those who can't sleep is that, being in the pill age, they might resort to taking a sleeping tablet to get to sleep. They'd be better off if they would learn how to relax. One way to relax is to go off by yourself, find a quiet place, sit down, and try and get your mind off the game. There's a lot of talk today about meditation and inner thinking, and I think there's much to be said for those methods. I think a lot of coaches make the mistake of stirring up

their players too much before a game, like old Knute Rockne of Notre Dame did with his famous fight talks. This is wrong, particularly where teen-agers are involved."

## OTHER TRAINING
## CONSIDERATIONS

1. Frequent health examinations are a must, and chest X-rays should be included.
2. Clean locker and shower rooms will help eliminate "athlete's foot" and other infections. Shower clogs for the athlete are an asset.
3. Clean clothing, especially a clean supporter and clean socks, helps prevent rashes and inflammations that could remove the player from training or competition.
4. Supervised heat lamp treatments and hot water whirlpool baths can hasten recovery from sprains, strains, and bruises.
5. A good text dealing with hygiene and injuries in the field of physical education and athletics should be studied.

## HOT WEATHER
## FOOTBALL HINTS

Early fall football practice is often held in extremely warm and humid weather in many sections of the United States. Under such conditions, special precau-

**Coach Knute Rockne**

tions should be observed. Otherwise, the athlete is subject to heat exhaustion (depletion of salt and water due to excessive sweating) and heat stroke (overheating due to breakdown of the sweating mechanism). Either condition can result in serious physical harm and even death. Both are preventable.

Following the suggestions below should help you to avoid ever experiencing heat exhaustion and heat stroke:

1. Have a checkup prior to the start of fall practice.
2. Be sure your coach schedules workouts during cooler morning and early evening hours.
3. Acclimate yourself to hot weather practice by carefully graduated practice schedules.
4. During workouts of an hour or more in hot weather, allow for rest periods of fifteen to thirty minutes.
5. Wear white clothing (to reflect heat) that is loose and comfortable (to prevent heat escape) and permeable to moisture (to allow heat loss via sweat).
6. Take extra salt and water in recommended amounts (intake at any one time should be held to one-half a water glass or less).
7. Watch yourself—and your fellow teammates—for signs of trouble, particularly those determined athletes who may not report discomfort.
8. Remember that the temperature and humidity and not the sun are the vital factors. Heat exhaustion and heat stroke can occur even in the shade.

# SHAPING UP: EXERCISE

## BASIC EXERCISES

Injuries are as old as football itself. Studies reveal that injured football players lose an average of 7.5 days of practice per season. (Any day a player cannot fully take part in practice is deemed a lost day.) Knee injuries account for 56.4 percent of the missed practice time, the average knee injury resulting in a loss of 8.8 days. The average shoulder injury loses the player 6.9 days, and the average ankle injury loses the player 5.9 days.

Since the prevention of injury is so closely related to conditioning—at all levels of the game—it is important for you to get and stay in condition. Here are a few basic exercises designed especially for younger players, whose bodies are just beginning to develop and flesh out:

*Pull-Ups.* For arm flexors, shoulders, and upper back. Hang from an overhead bar, arms fully extended and feet off the ground. Hands should be about shoulder width, palms facing away from the face. Pull up until your chin clears the bar, then lower all the way down. Do this three times daily, using two-thirds of your maximum effort. If, for example, the most pull-ups you can do at one time is six, then do three sets of four pull-ups per day.

*Sit-Ups.* For the abdominal muscles. Lie on your back, with knees raised, hands behind your head, and feet flat. Have a partner hold your feet as you sit up. Your goal should be two-thirds maximum effort, twice daily.

*Wall Sitting.* This exercise is designed to strengthen your upper leg and thigh muscles. Stand 1 to 2 feet (.3 to .6 m) from a wall, with your feet spread shoulder width. Now lower yourself to a sitting position, with your knees at a right angle to the wall. Lean motionless against the wall with your arms folded across your chest. Do this for ten seconds at a time, twice daily. Add five seconds each day, and try to reach thirty to sixty seconds.

*Leg Raises.* For upper legs, hips, and stomach muscles. Lie on either side with your head on your arm. Raise leg as far as possible (count one), hold for two seconds, lower leg to floor (count two). Set your goal for a count of fifty, two sets daily, each leg.

*Push-Ups.* This exercise bolsters your back, arms, chest, and shoulder muscles. Do it twice a day, two-thirds maximum. Support your body on your hands and toes, with your hands directly under your shoulders. Keep your body flat and rigid. Push up and down, gently touching your chest to the floor each time. Fingertip push-ups will strengthen your hands for better ball-handling.

*Jogging.* For heart, lungs, endurance, and muscle efficiency, running is still the best exercise. Start jogging at a comfortable pace that will cause your heart rate to increase to about 150 to 170 beats per minute. Jog for two minutes and then walk for thirty to sixty seconds. Repeat four to eight times. When you can easily handle eight of these timed jogging periods, lengthen each running period one minute, but keep the rest interval to thirty to sixty seconds. Follow this procedure until you can jog continuously for fifteen to twenty minutes. Set a personal goal of fifteen to twenty minutes of continuous jogging every other day.

*Jumping Jacks.* These help to coordinate the muscles in your upper back, shoulders, lower back, and legs. Start from a standing position, feet together, hands at sides. Kick your legs out to the side while touching your hands above your head (count one). Return to starting position (count two). Do two or three sets a day, working yourself up to a count of fifty.

*Rope Skipping.* This tunes up your agility, coordination, and timing. There are a lot of ways to skip rope: one foot, two feet, forward, backward, slow, fast, superfast. Set a goal of at least sixty seconds, nonstop, three times a day.

*Forward and Backward Running.* For explosive energy, speed, and running agility. Run hard for twenty seconds, then walk backward for thirty seconds; run for forty seconds, walk backward for thirty seconds. Rest three to five minutes. Repeat two more times. Run on days you don't jog. Work on increasing your speed.

## ISOMETRICS

Another excellent way to develop your body is with isometric contraction exercises. There are eight good, basic exercises you can work on both during the season and off-season. Each will help build up the large muscles of your body.

Start with about 50 percent of maximum effort and gradually increase the strength of the contraction. The gradual build-up of the contractions should take no more than three seconds and then be held for about twelve seconds. Each exercise should take about fifteen seconds altogether.

*Dead Lift.* This exercise is done by pulling against the bar at about knee-height, or just below the knees. Keep your back straight and bend your knees slightly. Your feet should be about a shoulder's width apart and the insteps of your feet placed directly under the bar. The dead lift is particularly good for the development of your back and shoulder muscles.

*Shoulder Shrug.* Stand up straight. Place the bar at a height where you can grab it when your arms are fully extended downward. Grip the bar with your hands about a shoulder's width apart. Now shrug your shoulders upward as hard as possible. This exercise will develop your shoulder muscles and the upper portion of the large trapezius muscles of the back and neck.

*High Press.* Set the bar about 4 inches (10 cm) below the height of your hands when your arms are fully extended overhead. Stand directly under the bar. Grasp the bar with your hands about a shoulder's width apart. Look straight ahead, tighten your leg, hip, and back muscles, and push on the bar as hard as you can. This exercise develops the pushing muscles on the back of your arms, shoulder and neck muscles, plus the back, abdominal wall, and legs.

*Leg Curl.* Lie down on your stomach on a bench with your knees extended just over the end of it. The bench is in front of the bar, with the bar set just high enough to hook your heels under it. Now try to bend your knees with the heels still hooked under the bar.

*Rise on Toes.* Adjust the bar to about 2 inches (5 cm) above the knees. Place yourself on a bench so that your knees are directly under the bar and your feet are directly under your knees. The lower leg should be perpendicular to the ground. Use a towel for padding between your knees and the bar. After you are in position, raise your heels off the floor, forcing your knees up against the bar. If you are in good condition you should be able to exert at least 1,000 pounds (450 kg) of force against the horizontal bar. It is recommended that on alternate days you change the position of your feet from pigeon toe to pointed out. This exercise will develop the muscles in the calves of your legs and feet. It will aid in the prevention of ankle and foot injuries and give you that explosive power needed in starting and running.

*Leg Press.* Lie on your back on a bench with your hips directly under the bar and your feet placed up against it. Your knees are at about a 150-degree angle. Your pelvis should be flat on the bench and your head should be held up off the surface, with your chin near your chest. Keeping your pelvis flat will prevent back strain; keeping your head up will prevent the blood from rushing to it. This is a very good exercise for developing maximum leg strength and power.

*Crushing Exercise.* Using a tackling dummy, put your shoulder against it and then encircle it with both arms so that they are almost head-high. Now pull the dummy against your shoulder in a crushing or hugging movement. This exercise will develop the muscles on the front of your arms and chest—muscles that are used to a great extent in tackling a ball-carrier. Both linemen and backfield men will find this an excellent exercise.

*Foot Flexor.* This exercise is done with the help of a partner. Sit on the ground, or on a bench, with your feet extended. Now have your partner hold the upper section of your feet in his hands to stop you from flexing your feet. Be sure he is holding on to the upper part of the feet. Do not have him exert pressure on the toes. This exercise will strengthen the muscles on the front of the leg and will reduce the incidence of shin splints, sprained ankles, and foot-arch trouble.

## WEIGHT-LIFTING

For years weight-lifting was feared as a dangerous way of building up the body. Then, several decades ago, all that changed. Some research physiologists claimed that their studies showed that weight-lifting might very well be the best training method for football players.

If you are normally healthy, the only danger in weight-lifting is in going too fast and too hard. You should base your program on the principle of *progressive* resistance, with slow, even-paced repetitions that gradually bring you through set stages of resistance overloads.

The system of progression is simple. Your muscles are trained to gradually do more and more work, so that injury or overwork is practically impossible. To develop strength and improve the muscle tone of the smaller muscle groups in your arms, shoulders, upper back, and chest, a progression from eight to twelve repetitions with a given weight is suggested before the weight is increased. That is, when beginning barbell or dumbbell training, or both, experiment to determine how much weight you can use to perform a given exercise eight times without stopping. With each training period, try to add a repetition. When you reach twelve, add 5 or 10 pounds (2.2 or 4.5 kg) and drop back to eight repetitions to begin the same upward progression of first adding repetitions and then adding more weight.

The larger leg and lower back muscles usually require more repetitions and can stand greater weight increases than the arms and upper body. In working the lower body and legs, do ten to fifteen or eighteen repetitions before adding 10 or 20 pounds (4.5 or 9 kg).

Since strength plays such a big part in football, helping to increase speed, balance, and coordination, and thus cutting down on costly injuries, you are urged to lift weights all year round. Multiple power racks, barbells, and dumbbells are the only equipment necessary. The rest is up to you. One word of caution, however: Allow for proper rest periods. Lift only every other day. Take a rest period between each lift of from three to five minutes. Warm up before each training session, doing parts of the exercise or using smaller weights and working up gradually to the complete movement.

Now, here are some exercises designed for overall benefit and to give tone to specific muscles.

*Military Press.* For shoulders and triceps. Pull the barbell to your upper chest, keeping your back straight by lowering your hips. Push overhead, lower to chest.

*Lateral Raise.* This exercise is designed to benefit the deltoid muscles. With your arms straight, knuckles up, raise the dumbbells from your thighs in an arc, meeting overhead.

*Wrist Curl.* This is for your forearm. First, grasp the barbell with your palms up and your arms on your thighs. Now, let the bell roll to your fingers and retrieve it.

*Alternate Press.* For arms and side muscles. Raise moderately heavy dumbbells to your shoulders, and then push overhead in an alternate seesaw action.

*Squat.* For thighs and hips. Place the barbell on

your shoulders at the back of your neck, keeping your back straight, chest high. Lower into a full squat and rise.

*Supine Press.* This exercise benefits your chest and triceps muscles. Simply push the barbell straight up from your chest until your arms lock.

*Pullover.* In this exercise you grasp a light-weight barbell with your arms straight behind your head, inhale, and lift up until the bell is over your chest. Exhale as the weight rises. This is a good exercise for chest expansion.

*Shoulder Shrug.* This is an excellent exercise for toughening the arms and shoulders. Lock your arms over your chest, take the barbell from a teammate, hold the position, then shrug your shoulders forward and upward.

*Curl.* To strengthen your biceps, arm, and forearm muscles, grasp the barbell, palms away from your legs. Now raise the bell until it is across your thighs, then to your chest in an arc.

## FOOTBALL INJURIES

Orthopedic surgeons and big-league trainers say that 60 to 70 percent of the chronic injuries they see in former college and pro football players might have been avoided had the players been properly treated at the time of the mishap.

Major-league trainer Gary Nicholson (Chicago Cubs, Seattle Mariners) blames part of the trouble on the athletes themselves.

"What really bugs me is when an athlete tries to hide his injury after he gets hurt. He doesn't get it taken care of early enough. He limps around playing hero, but by ignoring it the injury is prolonged. It doesn't heal properly, and, consequently, the player winds up with a gimpy knee or a bad shoulder or whatever. A lot of these old injuries are blamed on college and pro ball, whereas they actually happened in high school.

"Actually," Gary continued, "when we talk about football injuries, we should begin by talking about the *prevention* of injuries. The most formidable safeguard is a good conditioning program. You can't stress running, weight-lifting, and body-building exercises enough.

"As we learn more about athletic injuries, ice massage seems to be the most effective treatment yet for such routine aches as strains, sprains, bruises, and charley horses.

"As for tape, it depends on your philosophy and budget. Pro football teams use a lot of tape. In fact, some pro teams actually fine their players if they go onto the field without first being taped. You must realize that this athlete is a valuable piece of property, worth a lot of money. When he can't play, he costs the owner money. Tape is used to help prevent injury; it's like insurance. If I'm going to use tape, however, I'm going to use it *after* an injury occurs. I am a firm believer in exercise for strength.

"If your muscles are strong and you practice good conditioning principles, then you should never get injured. You'll learn that when you stay in sound shape you won't become sick as easily. You'll sleep better, study better, will have more energy. Here again you will come back off an injury much more quickly if the rest of your body is healthy. For example, if a player has a knee injury he will recover two, three, even four weeks sooner than, say, a person just off the street who suffers a similar injury. So stay in shape."

# SOME PRE-COLLEGE FOOTBALL NOTES

The late Coach Bernie Bierman, builder of national champions at the University of Minnesota in the 1930s and early 1940s, had certain rules he laid down to his Golden Gophers that still hold true today.

1. Enjoy football and give your best on every play.
2. To play your best, be in good shape, and have adequate rest before each game.
3. Do not place personal glory and success above the best interests of the team.
4. No smoking, no drinking.
5. Be calm and determined, not keyed up to a hysterical pitch for a game.
6. Develop speed, because it is essential to any style of play.
7. Work hard over a comparatively long period rather than squeezing in short, intensive drives during the heat of a season. This is the best way to develop.
8. Play hard, *clean* football.

## DON'T THINK PRO NOW

Mel Hein, one of the most respected names in the history of college and professional football, cautions

Pop Warner, one of football's
all-time coaching geniuses,
encouraged his players to play clean
—but hard—football. "There's no system
of play," he told them, "that substitutes
for knocking an opponent down."

you to take your time in deciding whether or not to make a career of football. Hein was an All-American center at Washington State, the star of the Cougars' 1931 Rose Bowl team. He was also All-Pro with the New York Giants for eight seasons in a row—and a member of both the college and pro Halls of Fame.

"In high school," Mel told me, "a boy should be thinking about a well-balanced, all-around program, not just football. His program should be designed to develop both mind and body. For example, he should get involved in another sport besides football to keep himself active during the off-season.

"I cannot caution high school athletes enough against thinking about professional football too soon. Wait until college. Once you have played several years of varsity ball there you'll know whether or not you are pro material. That's the logical time to make your decision. Your size and speed will have a lot to do with your decision, too. A 200-pound [90-kg] college tackle, for instance, will not survive the cut in pro ball. They like their linemen *big* there. Many backs and flankers can get by weighing 175 to 200 pounds [80 to 90 kg], but what they lack in size they make up for in speed and quickness."

Hein believes that one of the most common mistakes some high school players make is trying to tell the coach where to play them. Too many young players, he says, clamor to be running backs or tight ends—the "glamour" positions—because that's where all the publicity is. "But there are other positions where an average athlete can play, if he shows he has desire, the proper attitude, and team loyalty. Once a boy finds his position, then he must dedicate himself to making himself better. This means time, hard work, and patience."

Hein advises that you go to practice on the first day of fall workouts with an open mind. "Above all else," he warns, "avoid specialization at an early age. One of the hardest aspects of coaching youngsters is finding players who want to play in the line. So if they're really interested in playing football, then their best chance of making the varsity is in the line."

## SIZE—HOW IMPORTANT IS IT?

You are still a few years away from your full growth, and may be concerned over how much bigger you will get. Will you be large enough to attract college scouts?

Small football players have always been a part of the game. Tommy McDonald, the Philadelphia Eagles' explosive wide receiver of the 1950s, was 5-feet-9 (1.70 m). Jimmy Orr, another receiver for the Baltimore Colts and the Pittsburgh Steelers, was only 5-feet-10 (1.75 m). And Noland (Supergnat) Smith, who used to return kicks for the Kansas City Chiefs, was a mere 5-feet-6 (1.65 m).

These men were exceptions then, but they would not be today. In the past few years a substantial majority of the NFL teams have drafted at least one player

**Over left: Lynn Swann, the Pittsburgh Steelers' great pass-catcher, is only 5-feet-10-inches (1.75 m). Over right: Houston Oilers' Billy "White Shoes" Johnson (84), a fantastic kick-returner, is only 5-feet-9-inches (1.70 m).**

5-feet-10 (1.75 m) or shorter and 180 pounds (80 kg) or lighter. And the number of talented small players is growing all the time.

"I don't understand why people keep talking about size," Cleveland Browns running back Greg Pruitt complains. In the behemoth world of the NFL, Pruitt, at 5-feet-9 (1.70 m) and 190 pounds (86 kg), is more than middling small. From his first day in football as a seventh-grader—when a 4-feet-4-inch (1.3 m) school-mate looked down on him and dubbed him "Shorty"—Pruitt has been undersized and tremendously success-ful—an All-American at the University of Oklahoma and a Pro-Bowl star. Says Pruitt: "I've had to play at this size all my life. I've always been the smallest guy on the field. I've turned it into an advantage. I can position myself behind my blockers so that a defensive guy has to commit himself just to see where I am. It's a cat-and-mouse game. He shows up on the outside, I go inside. He shows up inside, I go outside."

The Baltimore Colts' Howard Stevens, 5-feet-5 (1.62 m), 162 pounds (72 kg), and the smallest man in the NFL, advises smaller players that the important thing "is to get the chance to show what you can do and not get written off by your coach on size alone. Then you've got to cash in on that chance, because as a small man, you may not get another."

No matter who their target is, little men can be big trouble. The Los Angeles Rams' Harold Jackson dreads a hit from small defensive backs: "When a bigger guy

**Cleveland Browns'
running back Greg Pruitt.**

Running back Terry Metcalf (21)
set an NFL record in 1975 for net
yardage gained by capitalizing on his
small size (5-feet-10-inches or 1.75 m):
"I'm smaller and harder to grab. If they
can't hit me, they can't hurt me," he says.

hits you, he just hits you enough to put you down. But those little guys are trying to take your head off; they really let down the boom on you."

## INSTRUCTIONAL
## FOOTBALL CAMPS

A growing part of pre-college football today is what are known as summer instructional camps. You see them advertised in *The Sporting News* every week. The more successful ones are held for three one-week sessions in late June and run until mid-July on both coasts and are supervised by highly competent coaching staffs.

These football camps are designed for boys between the ages of eight to eighteen. Each boy is grouped according to his ability, size, maturity, and previous football experience.

Instructors include junior high school, high school, and college coaches, along with many stars from pro football. Instruction ranges from practicing football fundamentals to developing advanced skills, and includes such activities as drills, conditioning, training methods, weights, isometrics, position play, films, chalk talks, and rules interpretation. Physical contact work is also offered on all age levels.

When you report to one of these instructional football camps, you will receive a schedule. The first part of that schedule will deal with fundamentals. For example, each defensive back works on his stance, footwork, tackling technique, etc., and then moves on against the linebackers to work on complete zone and man-to-man coverage. In your final days at camp, your instructors will emphasize coordinated teamwork— bringing all positions together into a unified group.

Complete offensive teams then practice against complete defensive units in both dummy and controlled contact scrimmages.

Other important subjects you will be taught include the prevention and care of injuries, running, weight-training, proper diet, proper attitude, spirit and desire, and such specialties as place-kicking, punting, and quarterbacking (stance, drop, set, throwing, release, ball-handling, footwork, faking strategy, reading defenses, option, and rollout).

A typical day's schedule goes something like this:

| | |
|---|---|
| 7:30 – 8 a.m. | — Running program. |
| 8:15 – 9:15 | — Breakfast. |
| 10:30 – 12 noon | — Morning workout: warm-up exercises, stretching, agility drills, offensive football (blocking, footwork, receiving, passing, and individual work). |
| 12:30 – 1:30 p.m. | — Lunch. |
| 1:30 – 2:30 | — Rest, digest, relax. |
| 2:30 – 2:45 | —"Chalk talk" and afternoon practice. |
| 2:45 – 3:15 | — Warm - up exercises, especially stretching, followed by running program, rope course, and quickness-reaction drills. |
| 3:15 – 4:30 | — Contact drills, position techniques (stance, assignments, movement, perimeter work in defensive, sets). Specialties: punting, place-kicking, holding, snapping, punt returns, special teams. |
| 4:30 – 6:30 | — Recreational time (swimming, tennis, hiking, weight-lifting, golf, volleyball, gymnastics). |

| 6:30 – 7:15 | — Dinner. |
| 7:30 – 8:30 | — Fun time: more games of your choice. |
| 8:30 – 9:30 | — Football films and talks by the pros. |
| 10:15 | — Lights out. |

Generally these summer football camps are well supervised. A live-in trainer and registered nurse are available on the grounds, and you will be required to undergo a pre-camp physical examination from your family doctor. You are also expected to supply your own equipment: shoulder pads, helmet, chin strap, pants, pads, cleats, mouthpiece, cup, and athletic supporter. If you don't have this gear, you may rent it at the camp.

Tuition averages around $195 per week, although special rates are available for day students and groups. Each camp conforms to the rules followed by your high school and junior high school football programs.

If you are among those who feel that football is your chance for future fame and fortune, then it may well be worth the $195 investment for the privilege of practicing before the critical eyes of topnotch coaches and professional players. You will be expected to practice hard and listen closely to everything they tell you. These camps do give you a chance to learn and develop. They also give you a good picture of football, its hopes, its spirit, its joys, its difficulties, and its dreams.

## FOOTBALL EQUIPMENT

Listen to what the 1977 Coach of the Year, the University of Washington's Don James, says about equipment:

"We have four full-time, qualified equipment people looking after our players. That's how much importance we put on proper equipment. Our biggest problem is with those players who want to sneak out on the practice field without all their uniform on. When we catch them we run them right back into the locker room. We *insist* that they suit up properly. They must wear everything. There are no exceptions. Some of them show up on the field with those really light shoes, with bad arch supports, and we quickly get them out of those, too. The two and three hours a day of constant pounding on Astro Turf is terribly hard on feet, so proper shoes are very important. For the best protection against injury, I tell players to always consider their own gear carefully. Does it fit them? Is it comfortable? Do they feel fully protected? I want them to speak up."

Here is a description of each piece of equipment you will be wearing when you go out for football:

*Thigh guard.* The heavy muscles on the front and outside of the thigh are protected by fiber or plastic shields, which are covered with foam rubber or quilted kapok. Each guard should rest fairly high on the thigh and fit snugly enough to prevent it from slipping out of place.

*Shoulder pads.* Shoulder pads are made up of several molded fiber pieces that are riveted or strapped together in such a way as to not hinder or restrict upward movement of the arms. The under surface of a shoulder pad is covered with a soft substance such as foam rubber kapok.

*Hip pads.* The hips, sacrum, and kidneys are protected by hip pads which are made of fiber and padding molded to fit the body. Body areas that must be well

**University of Washington's
Don James.**

covered are the top of the hip bone, the hip joint, and the sacrum and coccyx bones (center of the buttocks).

*Helmets.* Every player needs an excellent helmet. The most common type in use today is plastic and has molded ear pieces that protrude slightly to prevent undue pressure on the ear. This helmet features a web suspension on the inside, which fits over the head without allowing the helmet itself to touch the head except at the ears. A helmet should cover the base of the skull and protect the ears, temples, and forehead. It should not be too tight, but should feel comfortable and secure. A helmet that wobbles may be pulled off easily or rock down over the eyes, blocking vision.

*Mouthpiece.* Be sure to wear your mouthpiece on the field at all times. This device is responsible for cutting dental injuries down to practically zero. Credit must also go to the face bar. Together these items have helped tremendously in eliminating facial injuries.

*Shoes.* Because feet are the basis of the entire game, do not ignore the type of football shoes you wear. They must fit snugly and well.

## TIPS FROM THE TOP

Down through the years, athletes' formulas for success have varied. But most of their ideas still make good sense today. Here are how a few former champions claim you too can reach championship condition.

*Em Tunnell, New York Giants.* "Live clean, keep good hours, always hustle, and follow the advice of your coach and trainer. And then there's this tip my father gave me: 'Always regard yourself as equal or superior to your opponent—whether it be in sport or the game of life.' That was my motto and I did well by it."

*Al Demao, Washington Redskins.* "As long as you play football, give it your best shot. Listen to your coaches, be conscientious. To play football at any level, you'll have to be in top shape. I kept in A-1 condition by getting plenty of sleep, ate well, and drank lots of milk. I shunned cigarettes, trained diligently. Make up your mind right now that football is hard work—but it is worth it. In college, I started as a third-stringer, but by hard work and sheer determination I won myself a position on the varsity. I could have given up in my frosh year, but I didn't. I kept working harder and harder until, one day, I was on top. So the name of the game is hard work. It will carry you to whatever height you're set on. I really believe that."

*Charley Conerly, New York Giants.* "Regular eating habits consisted of a light breakfast and lunch, heavy dinner, with plenty of meat and milk. I was in bed nightly by 11 o'clock. I kept in shape by lots of running. If you're a running back, practice side-stepping, cutting and all phases of the running game. If you're an end, practice faking and all those little things that make a good, all-around end. Practice your position at all times. Listen to advice, as you can always improve yourself. Ask the older players about how they play their particular position. Be attentive, be alert."

*Frank Gifford, New York Giants.* "My biggest attribute was an incessant *desire* to make good in pro football. I always played to win. If you don't have that hunger for victory you won't win. My old college coach at Southern Cal, Jeff Cravath, taught me that you can do just about anything you desire—*if* you are willing to pay the price. The price is hard work, good everyday living habits, and determination. These ingredients will usually make a good athlete out of a fair one, and a great one out of a good one."

*Richard Todd, New York Jets.* "I made it a practice to stay in shape year-round. My advice to youngsters is to work yourselves into shape *gradually*. Start your preseason training and conditioning program early enough in the summer so that you won't have to rush it in order to be ready for opening day practice. Don't ignore injuries, no matter how slight. Take care of them immediately and thoroughly. Above all else, don't be too cocky. You might be good, but there is always someone out there who is better."

*Hugh Taylor, Washington Redskins.* "I usually got nine hours of sleep, 11 p.m. to 8 a.m. I started out the day with a breakfast of fruit juice, three poached eggs, and coffee. I spurned bacon because we practiced mornings, and physical activity and grease don't blend very well. For lunch I had a bowl of soup, a sandwich, and milk. My evening meal generally consisted of meat—steak, veal cutlet, or roast—and plenty of vegetables and milk. I never ate between meals, and I shunned sweets. Develop sound bathroom habits. I made it a habit to go to the toilet daily after breakfast. I believe this is very important to athletes, because a sluggish, constipated athlete is usually ill-tempered and not very alert. Plenty of water will help. Incidentally, don't abuse your body by filling it full of junk food. One last suggestion: Wear a smile on your face, at all times. No matter how angry or hurt you are, smile. I used to drive opponents crazy because they couldn't wipe the smile off my face."

**Richard Todd of the New York
Jets, seen here playing for
Alabama in the 1975 Sugar Bowl.**

# CHOOSING A COLLEGE AND WINNING A SCHOLARSHIP

There are about a million boys who play high school football annually, and about 200,000 of these are seniors. The senior high school produces the "blue-chip" players for the 125 or so colleges listed as major football powers by the National Collegiate Athletic Association (NCAA). It is safe to say that only about 3,750 of the 200,000 are given football scholarships by the major universities each year.

To qualify you must have the height, the weight, the agility, the extraordinary speed, and an appetite for hitting and being hit.

Officially, the NCAA rules state that a football scholarship is supposed to be limited to "tuition, books, room, and board." The candidate must also be eligible academically. That is, on the basis of his high school record, the boy must have done the equivalent of C work. Anything less than that makes him ineligible for an athletic scholarship. The candidate's standing can be measured any way his high school wishes: class rank, academic average, college board scores, and so on.

The active recruiting period at most colleges usually starts the week after the final game of the regular season, or roughly around December 1. Most high school coaches know soon enough if you are a college prospect. Either a coach or an enthusiastic alumnus will send off newspaper clippings about you to some college head coach.

In the spring of each year, hundreds of questionnaires are mailed out by assistant college coaches to high school coaches in every part of the country, asking if any members of their team are of big-time caliber. If so, the coach will fill out the questionnaire, noting down size, speed, academic standing, and whether the boy might be interested in playing ball at the sender's college. From the questionnaire, the college may put a boy on a "check further" list, and that boy will be evaluated again after he finishes his senior season.

College coaches broaden their picture of a prospect by studying film of the boy's high school games, talking to the boy on the phone, and visiting him in person. A high school coach, blinded by emotion and enthusiasm, may think a boy is a blue-chip prospect, when maybe he isn't. Or, as one college coach told me, "He may not realize what it takes to play big-time college football. He may not know how physically tough college football is, or how much concentration and dedication it takes."

The most useful tool in seeking the truth is film. Few prospects are signed without first checking their high school game films. What the college coach wants to know is, how does a lineman fire out and make his blocking contact? How does he control his feet? How does he use his hands on his defensive rush? How strong is he? Can he shuck off blockers? Can he strip interference? Can he handle double-teaming? A smart college coach can read the true meaning of a boy's game film and know immediately whether or not he wants to recruit him.

If you have genuine talent, the college will probably

know it early. Woody Hayes points out that the great prospects show their real ability by the time they are high school juniors.

## COLLEGE SCHOLARSHIPS

How often have you heard someone, maybe even yourself, say, "Who, me? I could never win a college scholarship. My grades aren't good enough. I'm not a star football player. So what's the use in trying?" The truth is, you probably *can* win a scholarship, if you only follow some of the suggestions listed below.

Each year hundreds of college scholarships, grants, loans, or part-time jobs go begging, merely because most kids don't know where or how to look for them. Finding a scholarship may be a little bit like playing hide-and-seek. You may have to look high and low before you locate it. But be persistent. If you really want to go to college there are a lot of people out there ready to help. However, it's up to you to make the first move. Here are some ideas on how to get started:

*Start with your high school counselor.* Drop by your counselor's office before the end of your junior year or at the beginning of your senior year. Your counselor can tell you about different state and federal programs designed to help you pay for your college education. Depending on your present financial need, the government may pay for all or part of your education. Also, ask your counselor about the National Merit Scholarship program.

**Coach Woody Hayes on the field with his players during the 1976 Rose Bowl game.**

*Write to different colleges.* Send a brief note of inquiry to several of the colleges that are of interest to you. Address your letter to the Admissions Office of each college, and ask for complete information on entrance requirements, tuition, room and board, and available financial assistance. Don't wait until the end of your senior year. Do it *now.*

*Check with your parents and other relatives.* Many commercial companies sponsor their own scholarship programs for sons, daughters, or close relatives of their employees. If a member of your family belongs to a labor union, this might be another source of financial aid. Also, different civic, fraternal, and religious groups offer scholarships based on qualities such as leadership, community service, or special creative talents. Ask your parents or family to check with their company, union, church, civic, or fraternal organization. The American Legion, Elks, Kiwanis, Lions, Masons, local Rotary Clubs, or Chambers of Commerce are especially active sources of student aid.

*You may qualify for social security, military, or minority benefits.* If you are the son or daughter of a retired, disabled, or deceased parent who was employed, you should contact the Social Security Administration about possible financial aid. Scholarships and loans are also available for dependents of active duty, retired, disabled, or deceased military personnel. Contact the branch of service that your parent served or is serving in, and ask for details. If you are a minority student, there are several state, federal, and private programs that offer assistance. Check with your school counselor, local minority organizations, and the colleges of your choice for information and application forms.

Remember—wherever you live, whatever your need, wherever you want to attend college, there is almost surely a source of financial aid available to you.

## RECRUITMENT

Major universities recruit in different ways. Some of them will try to influence you by the size of their facilities, the number of athletes who come to play for them, the number of times they get on television, or the number of intersectional games they play and the way they travel. But all have the full football scholarship— tuition, room and board, books and fees, practically your entire education—so choose according to the academic program you are looking for. At the same time, be on your best behavior, because the colleges are looking you over, too. They will be looking at your physical ability, as well as your high school academic record. They know that some athletes who come to them with high ratings physically will flunk out of school in the second year because they can't handle the classroom load. The competition among colleges, academically speaking, is higher today than ever before. The era of "soft" courses is over. College work is stiff, and if you aren't prepared to meet the standards you can forget about football.

Once you have made your decision, you must then file what is called a National Letter of Intent. You have probably heard of it before. Fill it out and mail it in to the college of your choice.

# COLLEGE FOOTBALL

On your first day at college, you may feel a bit lost, scared even. It's a lot different from high school.

At Pacific Lutheran University in Tacoma, Washington, Coach Frosty Westering, a member of Northwestern's 1949 Rose Bowl champions, starts each fall by picking his varsity lineup from those candidates who are in top shape.

"When the players check in, they don't depend on the coaching staff to get them in condition," says Frosty. "On the very first day of practice, we expect them to run a mile and three-quarters in twelve minutes. That's an excellent time. If they can't do it I know they haven't been paying the price for a winning season. We also check their hearts, their pulse beats. This tells us if they've been keeping their bodies in condition during the off-season. Other physical tests include a bench press, a thirty-second jump-rope, an agility sprint, and 20-yard and 40-yard dashes. The results tell us just how willing they are to play football.

"Then there's a second series of tests. It deals with fundamental skills. Fundamentals are the most important skills in football—blocking and tackling. To play this game you must be able to fire out and hit, to maintain contact on blocks, whether a body block or a shoulder block or a trap block. You've got to be able to react quickly, for modern defense is a contest of *reaction*—hit and react, hit and react.

"Essentially, we're looking for youngsters who are physically in shape, who possess the specific skills of their positions together with a desire to excel and encourage others.

"Maybe you were All-State in high school, a one-man gang, but all that is history by the time you arrive at college. Now you must learn to submerge yourself in among fifty or sixty other guys. Remember, the word *team* doesn't have an *I* in it. A successful team is composed of a group of fellows who are sharing some cooperative experiences, of giving a part of themselves. The coach is not so much interested in what you do on the field as he is in what the *team* as a whole does."

Thirty miles (47 km) north of Frosty Westering's campus, at the University of Washington, 1977's national Coach of the Year Don James talked about what freshmen should expect when they go from high school to college football. His football philosophy holds true in most areas of the country:

"We expect our players to be in shape when they come to fall practice. In fact, we mail out a summer conditioning program to each player. We start them in early June with a low-key fitness program. Each man is on his own. The program progresses from week to week, bringing them into mid-August in very good shape. We expect them to do a lot of leg work. We want them to run those miles. Football players like to avoid distance-running. They prefer the sprints. But jogging is invaluable to any training program.

"We also expect our athletes to do a lot of the quickness drills. A football play averages four seconds.

We, therefore, expect our players to spend fifteen minutes a day going full-speed for four seconds on the various quickness drills—a complete physical sellout for four seconds. That's a whale of a workout, if they'll do it. There's nothing easy about quickness drills. We also do a lot of weight-lifting in our program: bench press, overhead press, the squats, etc.

"In the summer, we send a letter to each player advising him what to do. Those letters go out every other week, along with a card for the players to fill out and return. The card informs us what they are doing to keep in shape. For example, on Tuesday evening, after dinner, the player rests for an hour, then goes out and jogs 2 miles [3.1 km]. He climaxes the workout with ten 40-yard [36.5 m] dashes. It's a program designed to get the players into shape without requiring several hours a day of their time. If the guys fail to return the cards we send them semi-monthly, then we get on the horn and call them.

"Most major universities—Washington among them —have taken the preseason conditioning program one step further. We now have a *winter* fitness program. We try to take our players into both spring and fall practices in A-1 health. If you don't have these extended programs you're going to end up getting your athletes hurt. Most serious injuries in college football happen in the first week of spring and fall practices. So, like the pros, we keep them in shape year-round.

"One rule for a freshman coming into a major college football program is that while he should arrive with a desire to make the varsity, he must have the *patience* to wait for his turn to play regularly. If he has the skills, his time will come. I also advise freshmen to finish what they set out to do. Set some academic goals, like graduate in four years. Don't be a dropout.

"Sherman Smith, now an NFL star with the Seattle Seahawks, has some sound advice for college freshmen: In college [Miami of Ohio], Coach Bill Mallory told us that we were there, first, for an education, and, two, to play football—in that order. He made us hit the books. As a pro, my career can end any day, but they can't take my education away from me. Secure? There's no such thing in pro ball. To fire us up, Coach Jack Patera warns, 'We'll put up with you until we find someone to replace you.' "

"At the start of fall practice, I call all the freshmen together—just the freshmen—and talk to them about football and their studies. Actually, I deliver two lectures to them, one on football at the start of the season and one on academics after they have attended classes for a while. I try to paint a realistic picture for them. They have had a lot of success in high school football (that's why we recruited them) and some of them lack the patience to make the college varsity. They expect to be overnight sensations in major games.

"I tell them about a player we had at Florida State who didn't start on the varsity for four years. He was red-shirted for one season and then he played his fifth year, made All-America, and went on to play in the NFL for five more years. He got his law degree and built up a very successful practice. So there was an example of a young athlete who had goals and patience. The message to that story is, don't bail out. Your turn will come. Too many high school recruits seem to come to college with parachutes on their backs. If things don't go right they say to themselves that they are not being treated fairly by the coach and probably should leave the program. Listen, we do not expect freshmen to play regularly. We feel that any game time we get out of them is a bonus.

**Left: Sherman Smith is brought
down by Miami Dolphins' linebacker
Kim Bokamper during third-quarter
play in the Orange Bowl.
Above: Coach Jack Patera giving
Sherman Smith the game ball from a
game the Seahawks won in 1976.**

"The first question I ask my freshmen is, what are their academic objectives? What educational programs have they mapped out for themselves? Right away, a small percentage of them eliminate themselves from our program. If a player says he wants to study agriculture, for example, and we don't have it, then we advise him to enroll at a college specializing in that field. We're fortunate at Washington (enrollment 37,000) in that we have a broad-based curriculum and can accommodate most athletes, even with exotic courses such as marine biology, fisheries, and forestry. We determine what they want and then as we go into each player's home we attempt to sell our academic counseling program. This is the key, our academic counseling program. We have a full-time counselor in charge of the program. It is her responsibility to keep an eye on the players' grades and work with them. At the beginning of each quarter, she helps them choose a curriculum, get registered, and keep up their grades. I require that our players attend a regular study table in the fall evenings. We have tutors, we have study tables, we require them to attend class regularly, and we follow up and make sure they do it all.

"Everybody talks about the marginal student-athlete. At Washington, if a boy appears he's going to be marginal, we do one of two things. We either reject him or have him tested. For example, we had two high school football prospects we interviewed who were very questionable academically. We just didn't think they could do college work and stay eligible for football. They fooled us. They went to another conference school, got passing grades, and wound up playing against us. So we sometimes miss the boat.

"On our team, we pick roommates. We try to match

our scholars with the student-athlete who has poor study habits, hoping it will rub off. That's what the great Knute Rockne did at Notre Dame. It's nothing new.

"I have a two-year live-on-campus policy for all my players who are receiving a football scholarship. If I'm paying their way through school, then they must obey. They are free to select the type of quarters—dormitory, fraternity, whatever—but it must be on campus and for two years. What I try to do is eliminate the travel problems, the parking problems—and I want a structured food program for them. Basically, I want my football players to become college students. After two years, if they want to move off campus and have the approval of their parents, they are free to do so. Unlike some major universities, we do not have an athletic dorm. We spread our athletes around the campus in a series of dorms. We try to encourage them *not* to live together. It broadens them to live among the rest of the student population.

"We find out a lot about high school recruits even before they come to us. We spend many hours talking to their high school coaches. We ask a lot of questions. 'Will he be a great college player?' 'Is the potential there?' 'Is he willing to play any position to help our team?' 'Will he accept harsh criticism?' 'Is he a good citizen?' 'Is he a good leader?' 'Will he crack the books, stay eligible?' 'Will he accept coaching?' 'OK, maybe he's a marginal student in the classroom—but what sort of student is he in football?' If the coach is candid with us and says the boy is smart in the classroom but dumb on the football field, then we probably won't recruit him.

"In three years at Washington, we have lettered twenty freshmen. That will give you an idea of what we think of first-year men and how times have changed.

And yet, the NCAA has cut our numbers. They have cut us down from sixty, fifty, forty freshmen to thirty. Most coaches average probably twenty-eight recruits. In the Pac-10, we are allowed a total of ninety football scholarships, whereas the national average is ninety-five. In the old days, there was no ceiling—it was what you could afford. The college squads are not as large as they used to be. This means we must be much more careful about the high school graduates we select. We recruit players from all over America. In 1978, we went after high school stars in Pennsylvania, New York, Virginia, Michigan, Kansas, Hawaii, Oregon, Idaho, California, and Washington. We go after the same kinds of players as Woody Hayes does at Ohio State. We have a whole page of criteria. We evaluate high school prospects much the way the Dallas Cowboys scout collegians. That is, we take the biggest tight end in a league, the smallest tight end, and the average tight end. We take the weight and average it, we take the speed, and we provide a point scheme for all these —we just don't put many marginally sized people on our list of possible candidates. But if we do decide to take a small, fast running back, then he must make up for lack of size with something extraordinary: extra speed, quickness, agility, something.

"What about training table? All high school recruits want to know about the food situation. The football scholarship each player receives stipulates a food program. During preseason practice and until school opens, we feed our players three meals a day. But once school begins, then we feed them just the evening meal. They eat the other two meals at their living quarters. Most major schools follow a similar plan. We have a professional nutritionist who supervises our training table meals. We discourage junk food.

"When one of my players becomes a senior and starts thinking about a career in pro football, I bring him into my office and alert him to the restrictions. He's not allowed, for instance, to sign with an agent until he completes his college eligibility. But once that is used up, I can tell him of the agents I know and advise him which to contact. As a matter of fact, I have a phone message on my desk right now for one of my graduating seniors to contact a certain agent. He has a choice of either playing pro ball in Canada, or in the NFL. I'll give him my opinion as to what I think he ought to do, but it will be his decision.

"Semipro football leagues? I really can't recommend semipro ball for college players who do not go on to the established NFL or Canadian league. The liability, the high cost of insurance, the risk of permanent injury is simply too great. Semipro players are not in the best of physical condition. Facilities and equipment and medical supervision are not the best. Football has become so costly that the risks of semipro football just aren't worth it. There are so many better ways for an ex-football player to stay active after college—jogging, tennis, golf, bowling, and weight-lifting, to name a few. No, if you don't make the big leagues, get out of football."

# THE PROFESSIONAL APPROACH

On some pro teams—not all—the players tend to think for themselves, and talk and act differently from when they played college football. They regard their coach as just another coach drawing Xs and Os on the blackboard. He'll be second-guessed or even mocked by the team because that's the way pro football is.

Pro football players are physically tough; some are even abrasive and coarse.

In a nutshell, pro football is jungle warfare. Be ready to go to war when you put on that pro uniform for the first time.

"I'm going to push you and push you and push you because I get paid to win and so do you," the late Vince Lombardi often exhorted his players. "Football is a violent game. To play it you have to be tough. Physically tough and mentally tough. You must have pride, because when two teams meet that are equal in ability and execution it's the team that has pride that wins."

Oakland Coach John Madden ranks simple pride as the first quality that makes a player a winner. He tells his rookies when they first report to him, "You must have such a desire to excel that you'll take enormous pains. You'll work out beyond what is demanded, build your body during the off-season, guard your weight and study the problems of your position."

A former schoolteacher with a master's degree—a pro coach who got his Raiders to the NFL play-offs seven times in eight years—Madden places toughness as the second quality for winning football. "By that I mean," he says, "doing what the job requires without worrying about the physical consequences. A wide receiver will make the catch, untroubled by the possibility of getting blindsided. A quarterback will hold the ball until the final instant, knowing the rushers will flatten him. The winning player has no fear of doing what must be done in order to be great."

Madden outlines a third quality as self-motivation. "I coached an All-Star game one year," he remembers. "We had on our squad the finest players in the American Conference. Each, I found, was self-starting. Each drove himself hard, showed up on time, learned the plays without prodding from the staff. I sponsored a buffet breakfast each morning at 8:30 for nothing more than talking football. All but just a handful joined every session. If a player can't motivate himself, it isn't likely that a coach can motivate him, either."

Finally, Madden says, "high intelligence" is required of a winning player. He said he defines intelligence as the ability to absorb information. "If the coaching staff can't get information to the players, you can't win," he points out. "We lean to the overload theory, meaning we give our players more information than often is necessary. But we win because we have people able to soak it up."

Coaching at his peak at Green Bay, Lombardi observed one day that his team was successful because of its ability to recruit "Packer types." It turned out that he meant players who were willing to adjust to his personality.

"I would be scared to death to try to get players to adjust to my personality," says John Madden. "When you change a player as a person, you also may be changing him as a player. It may be his original frame of mind that's making him good."

For most rookies, the transition period from college football to the NFL is tricky. Dick Jauron, who went from Yale to the Detroit Lions, remembers how the professionals seemed a little bit bigger, faster, and stronger than the collegians. "The football field seemed to shrink," he said. "The people on it took up so much more room." Another Old Eli, Calvin Hill, who starred for both Dallas and the Washington Redskins, recalls that his biggest surprise going into pro football was how much time he suddenly had to concentrate on the game. "It seemed such a luxury," he said. "At Yale you had two hours of football, and that was all, and then you had to start thinking whether the Civil War was inevitable, because that was what you were going to be quizzed on in a classroom."

In college you are asked to split yourself between the game and an education. But in professional football you are there exclusively to play as well as your abilities will allow.

For those of you who are preparing yourselves for careers in professional football, you would do well to listen to John Thompson, General Manager of the Seattle Seahawks, the most successful first-year expansion team in NFL history. Before coming to Seattle, John was the first full-time executive director of the NFL's

**Lions' Dick Jauron (26) in a
game against the Cleveland Browns.**

Management Council, the collective bargaining agent of the league's clubs. He also served as Assistant General Manager of the Minnesota Vikings. Recently, he talked to me about pro football as a career.

"There is nothing magical about what we look for in football prospects," John said. "When we go into the draft, we look for ability. We look for size, speed, agility, attitude, *character.* We, as all pro teams do, have scouts out all the time measuring the potential of college prospects. We time them, we know their weight, we have it down right to an eighth of an inch how tall they are. We know their speed in the 40-yard dash. We literally have a whole library of files on all the leading draft choices in the country.

"Our scouting staff has certain minimums by which we judge college players. We don't draft a boy unless he meets those minimums. We put a lot of stress on character and intelligence. We get this information from many sources—from the coaches, the trainers, the equipment managers—from the people who know the player best. We talk to the player himself, his teammates, his parents. Our job, before drafting him, is to know as much about the prospect as possible. There's no way he can bluff his way into our organization. We don't expect our players to be angels, but they must meet certain standards.

"Some small-college players may think they are overlooked by pro scouts, but they aren't. They are not automatically out of it at all. There are a lot of players from small schools who make the NFL grade. Look at the NFL rosters. There are dozens and dozens of

**Calvin Hill (35) in action
against the New York Jets.**

athletes listed from obscure colleges. So we look very carefully at the small-college market. Of course, a scout must project more when scouting those teams, because the players don't get as much personalized in-depth coaching as major college players. The coaching staffs are so much smaller. Another factor we take into consideration is that the small colleges play a softer schedule."

As soon as possible after the annual college draft, the Seattle Seahawks bring in all of their draft choices and free agents for a three-day orientation meeting. All are given physicals and the team trainers examine them. If any of them is overweight he has about six to eight weeks to get in shape for training camp in mid-July.

The first things the players receive when they get to training camp are the play books. Play books are heavy, stiff-covered loose-leaf notebooks, one for the offensive team, and one for the defensive. Each has index tabs listing such categories as screens, goal line, double-wings, and, in the back, blank pages for diagraming plays. The plays are drawn on the blackboard or thrown up on a screen by a projector for the players to copy down—the theory being that the assignments on a given play will be remembered better by having the players draw them into their own textbook.

Generally, the book for the offense is arranged by topics in the order of importance. Its first page, say, leads off with the heading "Two Minutes," and a first paragraph which reads: "Probably the most important part of a ball game is two minutes to go in either half. It is not only imperative for the team captain to know when time is out, and whether the clock starts with the snap or with the referee's whistle, but for each individual also.

**John Thompson, General Manager
of the Seattle Seahawks.**

Time-outs must be saved for these periods. A team that can handle itself through this period without confusion and frustration will be the champion."

Another category is "Third Down Situation." The text will begin: "The ability of a team to succeed on third down (either offensively or defensively) is the key to winning football . . . the good clubs in the league are the ones who excel on third down situations."

A third category of importance runs under the heading "Severe Penalties and Their Avoidance." First on the list is "Running into Kicker." The text warns: "A foul is often called if you just touch the kicker. This penalty is unpardonable." Also high on the list is "offside or holding on fourth down kicks," about which the text comments coldly, "There is no excuse for this foul."

Other than an index of "basic terminology," there is not usually much else in the offense book. The rest of the pages are blank and are for diagraming plays. Obviously, the book increases in content and value as you diagram your plays. Several new ones are taught at each evening class, so that by the time the training season is over almost a hundred plays will be drawn into the play book. Naturally, the penalty for losing your play book is high—one club imposes a $1,500 fine.

The defensive book is more interesting. Besides the usual warnings about penalties, and the importance of the third down and playing superior football for the last two minutes of each half, some play books include page after page of statistics, graphs, and charts, and a long section showing assignments for individual players against specific offensive plays. Football fans might not understand much of what is in this book.

What else should a rookie expect when he first reports to preseason camp? For the first several weeks he will have to practice twice a day, morning and afternoon, because the coaches want to know who is "durable." Later, the team will practice in the morning and attend team meetings in the afternoon and at night. The rookie's greatest enemy will be boredom, the aimless standing around that leads to mental flatness. Some coaches try to alleviate team boredom by pouring on the work and a lot of screaming. Lombardi was one of those who poured it on. He wouldn't stop until everybody was bushed.

"The name of the game is to play when you're hurt," Lombardi told his players. "What you need in football is your legs. Shoulders and ribs, they hurt when you get hit there again, but you don't need them to do your job. If you're a pro you can play hurt."

Times change. Life for a rookie at training camp today involves less nonsense than it did a decade ago. Rookies don't bow to veterans with "Yes, sir" and "No, sir" so much anymore. A lot of rookies come equipped with big egos, big money, and big reputations, and they simply refuse to put up with any nonsense.

It wasn't very many years ago that a rookie was given the cold shoulder by veterans. He couldn't count on much help from them. Alex Karras, an All-Pro defensive tackle at Detroit, remembers the first NFL game he started. It was against the Cleveland Browns. The Browns had an offensive guard named Harold Bradley. Bradley was a regular big buster of a guy with wrestler's muscles and a mean disposition. So Alex went to Gil Mains, his predecessor on the Lions, for advice. He was embarrassed and afraid Gil would think he was trying to take his job. But to Alex, it was a question of survival. He asked Gil, "What can I expect?" Gil started talking about Bradley. "Alex," he said, "he's probably the strongest guard I've ever seen in my life. He's going to kill you. You're not going to get past him. He's going to make you look foolish." Well, *that* wasn't the sort of stuff Alex wanted to hear. He began thinking of leaving camp.

Didn't Gil Mains give Karras any advice? Yes. "Never worry about traps," Gil told him. "They never trap." So when Alex got into the game, Bradley and the Browns trapped him forty-three times.

"That was typical," Alex Karras said. "Those old-timers on the team really made you work things out for yourself. It wasn't easy, but maybe you were the better for it."

When a rookie gets to training camp, there's one thing he can count on: competition. Usually, he will be competing against twelve draft choices, twenty-five to forty free agents, plus forty-plus veterans from the season before. To cut the odds against him, he'd better be in shape. That means training on his own during winter and spring, or else he's going to be at a big disadvantage.

"The tough, physical part of pro football is the training camp," warns John Thompson. "Once the regular season begins, the players spend most of the time in the classroom. A typical week during the season runs something as follows:

"Mondays—trainers examine bumps and bruises; review film of previous day's game; a little jogging around the practice field to loosen up.

"Tuesdays—day off; coaches prepare upcoming game plan.

"Wednesdays—heavy work day; players on practice field for two hours; spend equal amount of time in the classroom, boning up for next game.

"Thursdays—same as Wednesday.

"Fridays—same as Wednesday and Thursday.

"Then there's Saturday. If the next game is away,

then Saturday is a travel day. Let's say the game is at Cincinnati. The players' itinerary is as follows:

"Saturday, 9 a.m.—Practice at Kirkland, emphasis on the special teams.

"1 p.m.—Alaska Airlines Charter Flight No. 534 departs for Cincinnati from Seattle–Tacoma International Airport.

"8 p.m. (EDT)—Arrive in Cincinnati.

"9 p.m.—Dinner, followed by team meeting. Players have their choice of either prime rib or fish for dinner. Prime rib is the favorite.

"11 p.m.—Curfew.

"Sunday, 7:45 a.m.—Wake-up call.

"8:30 a.m.—Pregame meal, followed by taping. Breakfast consists of an eight-ounce steak and eggs and cereal.

"11:40 a.m.—Bus departs motel for stadium.

"1 p.m.—Kickoff.

"6 p.m.—Plane departs Cincinnati for Seattle. This is approximately two hours after the game ends.

"It is true what Norm Van Brocklin says about pro football being a tough way to make a buck, but if you make an NFL team the rewards can be mind-boggling. Here is a breakdown of salary figures that NFL players made in 1978:

| POSITION | PLAYERS | AVERAGE SALARY |
| --- | --- | --- |
| Quarterbacks | 88 | $89,354 |
| Running Backs | 182 | $60,414 |
| Receivers | 214 | $53,760 |
| Offensive Linemen | 280 | $52,250 |
| Defensive Linemen | 208 | $59,644 |
| Linebackers | 220 | $50,416 |
| Defensive Backs | 225 | $47,403 |
| Kickers | 59 | $41,506 |

"Our salaries don't compare with pro basketball, but of the 1,476 players who performed in the NFL when this study was made, the average salary was $55,288.

"Today, there are all sorts of incentive bonuses on top of a player's regular salary. This is very common in the NFL, but outlawed in major-league baseball. Football bonuses are given to players for notching a certain percentage of game time, for making so many yards in a season, for completing so many passes, for catching so many passes—there are all varieties of incentive bonuses written into a player's contract. A lot of them are based on team performance. As a team, the Seahawks do not believe in individual statistics. We do not use them in granting our bonuses. Some teams do, but we prefer giving bonuses for *team* play.

"If you can qualify for one of the NFL teams, a financially secure life is waiting for you. The career of a pro football athlete is considerably longer than it was ten years ago. Not only will you be eligible for an attractive life and medical insurance program, there is also an excellent pension plan, better even than the pension benefits that U.S. Steel and General Motors give their chief executives. About four years ago, for example, I sat down and figured out that had there been a pension plan when George Blanda first came into the NFL—at the salary levels we're now talking about—he could have started drawing a pension of between $85,000 and $90,000 a year at age sixty-five. Today, a retired NFL player can begin drawing his pension as early as forty-five; most start at fifty-five. We

**Former coach
Norm Van Brocklin.**

now have an agreement with the players' union that when a player retires from pro football he may take 25 percent of whatever money is accumulated for him in the pension plan. This is to help him bridge his career from football to the outside world."

For those of you who are drafted by one of the NFL teams, your first obligation to yourself is to get an established agent to represent you in contractual negotiations. There are good as well as bad agents. Be careful. But, you ask, where do you find an agent? Usually, *they* will find *you*. However, should an agent not come to you, then turn to your college coach for help. He is in a position to give you excellent advice. He will know of a good agent, or a local attorney, who can help you.

"Often it's a local attorney who negotiates the terms of a contract for a rookie, and many times he's just as good a bargainer as an agent," says John Thompson. "He's a friend of the college where the athlete played football, and he'll look out for the boy. The Players Association also has been weeding out the bad agents and steering rookies to the good ones. They'll be happy to furnish draftees with the names of reputable agents."

Beginning in 1978, the Seattle Seahawks started holding classes for the players, the players' wives, and the administrative staff on how to invest their earnings. The club brought in an expert—at its own expense—to conduct the seminar. He was not selling anything. All he was doing was teaching a class in how to plan for the future.

"It's very important for our players, who are making such good money, to know how to handle their income, because at the end of their playing days they are suddenly going to be thrown into a primary career at substantially less pay," John Thompson points out. "We are simply preparing them for the adjustment. We want to broaden their financial background and help them to invest their earnings wisely. We encourage them to start planning now for that time when they leave football."

During the off-season, NFL team executives push their players to find jobs, stay active, and not just sit around growing hog-fat. John Thompson's advice is for them to get into a line of work that they intend to pursue after they retire from football.

"Here's something else rookies should be thinking about. We encourage all our players to get involved in the community. Not all do, but most. They do a lot of public speaking, a lot of charity work. From a selfish point of view, that's good for them, because they meet many of the leaders of the community who become impressed with them. Pro athletes have many more doors open to them than the average person, but once they get through the door they must prove themselves. They have advantages, but they must spend those advantages wisely. Otherwise, it's all lost."

# THE HIGHS AND LOWS
# OF THE GAME

Reasons vary as to why so many college men go on to play professional football. I once put the question to the late Dr. Wilbur H. S. Bohm, who served for years as chief trainer of the Washington Redskins and then the New York football Giants, and he said, "Because they want to be heroes. Sure they do. They play pro football to be recognized by the one man they learn to respect—the head coach. And they play it so they can see it in themselves. The greatest moment for some of them is when they walk into the locker room after they've won and have had a good day personally. They might have been beat up and bruised, but they didn't show pain. They looked like they were feeling great."

One NFL veteran said he played simply because he enjoyed football. "Money, yes, and the recognition, too. Why does anybody play? Well, first to prove to him-

**Quarterback Ron Jaworski experiencing one of the lows of the game. His team, though the favorite, has just been upset by the Dallas Cowboys in the 1976 Super Bowl.**

self that he can do it, second to prove to the guy next door he can do it, third because he enjoys it, and fourth for the money. Yet I've learned some things from the game I'm grateful for. It's funny, here I am engaged in the most violent profession there is, but I've learned from football to be a more peaceful, tolerant sort of person. At first I refused to share a dining table with black guys in camp. I'd never sat with a black man before. Then suddenly I was sitting with them and finding out all kinds of things I never got a chance to find out down home. These were fine people, just regular guys, and if it hadn't been for pro ball, I'd have never known that."

A. D. Whitfield, who played for the Redskins when Vince Lombardi coached them, had a theory about professional football. "It isn't like everyday life," he said. "In life you can make your own choices. You can say, 'Gee, this isn't right,' or 'Gee, this is.' But not in football. There's only one choice, and the coach makes it," Whitfield said. "Football makes a man mature late. You're twenty-five, thirty, sometimes thirty-five years of age before you go out in the world and are in charge of yourself and learn something. It's that way everywhere in football."

Another of the Redskins, Flea Roberts, compared football to prizefighting. "Football is an emotional game, like being in the prize ring," he said. "In football you got to hit a guy to wrack him up. You just hit him as hard as you know how. You don't want to hurt him, but you can't afford to hit him and let him run right on past you. So where do you draw the line between a

**A. D. Whitfield: "Football makes a man mature late."**

game and barbarism? You got to just slam in there and try and knock his block off: that's it, that's the only line there is."

When quarterback Gary Beban first went into pro football, he said it was scary to think about a normal life. "We're basically working off our bodies," the former All-American said. "In the real world your body doesn't matter; you've got to work off your mind, your personality, yourself."

Ray Schoenke, who was a lineman for the Redskins, believes it is time and luck that makes or breaks a football career. "Lombardi felt that Willy Banks could be an All-Pro guard, and he was right," Schoenke said. "Willy had all the potential, he was tough and he was quick. But he hurt his ankle, and that was bad luck. Then he had to play on it against Mean Joe Greene in Pittsburgh and Billy Ray Smith in Baltimore, and they stomped all over him—and that was the worst possible timing for a string of bad luck. So Willy was benched, and I was there. Once things go sour for you in pro football they're hard to set right. You're rejected, labeled as a loser. I know the feeling, it happened to me enough."

"I don't know what the word is for the feeling you're supposed to have about your team," said Pat Fisher. Pat was exceptionally small for a pro cornerback, but a bulldog of a player, as tenacious and pugnacious as the lines on his face, with his broken nose and determined jaw. "Respect is not quite it. There's a paradox about it. I'll have to admit it. If you can be traded to help the team, then bam, you're gone. Yet, you're supposed to have loyalty toward the team and the coach, and you ask, where is the loyalty that's supposed to be flowing back to me? That's a paradox."

I once asked a member of the Green Bay Packers what thoughts he had beyond pro football. Did he have any idea what he wanted to do?

"No," he said. "When it comes, it comes. Then it will be a challenge to find another career, another something to commit myself to. Being a pro athlete is a unique situation. In some ways it's unfair. You come out of school and succeed in a hurry, and then it's over. And you're still young."

Norm Evans, an All-Pro offensive tackle with the Miami Dolphins in the days when they were winning Super Bowls, decided when he hurt his knee in 1969 that he would never again complain about being a pro football player. "I'm human—certain things about football get to me," he admitted. "But when I had to spend six weeks in a cast, first on my back, then sitting down, then standing on the sideline, it nearly wiped me out. I almost went out of my mind. I promised myself that when I didn't want to play any longer, I'd just quit. I wouldn't go around bellyaching about football. I'd just get out. I wasn't going to kick a game that had put so much into my life."

Jerry Mays, a good defensive end for the Kansas City Chiefs when they defeated Minnesota, 23–7, in Super Bowl IV, tried going into the construction business one winter. The difference between playing pro football and being out there all alone in the business world shocked Jerry. "What they ought to do is make every college player serve a year in another line of work before he even tries pro football," Mays said. "Then he'd know what the *real* world is like. In how many other businesses can a man make up to six figures for six months of work and still get the emotional highs that football gives?"

Sonny Jurgensen, the old quarterback, says that going into pro football can be a tragedy. "Sometimes I wonder what's on a man's mind starting out all over again, trying to find something new to do with his life. Yet, all considered, football is still a great profession. The competitiveness of it, being part of a club of men who've made it all the way through. You can't regret that."

Good luck.

# INDEX

Kickers, 71
Kidney damage, 11
Knee injury, 25

Lateral raise, 23
Leg curl, 20
Leg press, 21
Leg raises, 18
Linebacker, 5, 35, 71
Lineman, 28, 45
Lombardi, Vince, 4–7, 60–62, 69, 79–80
Los Angeles Rams, 7, 32, 35

McDonald, Tommy, 29
Madden, John, 60–62
Mains, Gil, 69–70
Mallory, Bill, 53
Man-to-man coverage, 35
Mays, Jerry, 81
Medical insurance, 73
Meditation, 13, 15
Mental conditioning, 13, 15–16, 60
Metcalf, Terry, 34
Miami Dolphins, 81
Military press, 23
Minnesota Vikings, 65
Mouthpiece, 40
Muscle tone, 22

Namath, Joe, 3
National Collegiate Athletic Association, 44

National Football League, 5–6, 29, 32, 53, 59, 61–62, 65, 71, 73
National Letter of Intent, 49
National Merit Scholarship, 46
New York Giants, 40–41, 76
Nicholson, Gary, 11–12, 24–25
Notre Dame, 15, 57
Nutrition, 7–8, 10–12, 58

Offense, 36, 66–68
Offensive guard, 69
Offside, 68
Ohio State, 58
Orr, Jimmy, 29
Overhead press, 52
Overload theory, 61

Pacific Lutheran University, 11, 50
Passing, 36
Patera, Jack, 53, 55
Penalties, 68
Philadelphia Eagles, 29
Physical ability, 1, 12
Pittsburgh Steelers, 29
Place kicking, 36
Plays, 6, 51, 66–68
Precollege football, 35–37
Preseason training, 6, 43, 52, 68–69

# ABOUT THE AUTHOR

Starting as a sportswriter on Portland's *The Oregonian* when he was fresh out of Washington State University in 1947, John McCallum later spent twelve years covering major-league sports for national magazines and for the *NEA Syndicate* in New York City. A contributor to the *Encyclopaedia Britannica,* John is the author of twenty-seven books, among them *College Football, U.S.A.,* the official book of the National Football Foundation and Hall of Fame; *Ty Cobb,* a Sports Illustrated Book Club selection; and *The World Heavyweight Boxing Championship: A History,* a Literary Guild selection. Mr. McCallum now lives in Tacoma, Washington.

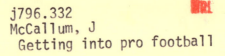